climb
and
chasm

my debut poetry collection

an arc of expressed thought
spanning the chasm of the abysmal
and the climb of ascension

follow me on social media
@posidovepen

climb and chasm

j.p. dove

climb and chasm © 2025 by J.P. Dove. All rights reserved.

No part of this publication may be reproduced, distributed, or transmitted in any form or by any means, without the prior written consent of the publisher, except in the case of reprints in the contexts of reviews and noncommercial uses permitted by copyright law. Any person who commits any unauthorized act will be held liable to criminal prosecution and civil claims. For permission requests, contact the publisher at the email address listed below.

Published by:

PosiDove Pen Press
Eugene, Oregon 97404
info@posidovepenpress.com

www.posidovepenpress.com

www.jpdove.com

Paperback ISBN: 979-8-9922570-0-7

E-Book ISBN: 979-8-9922570-1-4

Library of Congress Control Number: 2025900232

Cover Design by J.P. Dove

First Printing Edition 2025

Quantity sales are available for schools, retailers, and libraries at www.ingramcontent.com

at my highest

to all
who've
seen me
or been me

and my lowest

through peaks and valleys
across deluge and oasis
ink maps my journey
may these words
stir your soul

-j.p. dove

the contents of my heart

the abyss 1
the axis 21
the ascent 41
the apex ....…......................... 61

the abyss

oftentimes i sit and wonder
the lengths my heart will go
to reach the point of met desires
i'd surely like to know

how many storms and fires
until my heart's asunder?

-sacrificial serenity

if i could unzip my skin
like a sweater—

i'd hang it in the closet for months
stuff a few mothballs in my pockets
so i don't get chewed up
any more than i'm used to

would i need to moisturize it
like leather—
to keep from drying up?

if i could unzip my skin
i'd try on another sweater—

one sweeter than mine
not achy or weathered

and i'd probably run away
to hide like jinn do

-but would you try me on for size?

j.p. dove

sleep calls to me
like a lost friend
i yearn for its touch
to feel its warm breath
yet it does not come
and my eyes stay
op en

-a dash of insomnia

perilous thoughts
dragging their feet
begin to crawl into
my field of vision
walking into doors
of ill perspectives

speed intensifies
as if malice could
run into the rooms
making up my mind
to stir volatile volcanic
eruptions of emotion
trepidous tornadoes
of cyclical thought

how *dangerous* it is
to give away
your power
so freely

-*anger's.. gift?*

j.p. dove

burn me down
loose fireworks
in dry forest beds

i'm out of control

you light my fuse
and run away
i see red
and

                    e
     x   d
-e   p   o
       l

climb and chasm

cascading
formidable heights
tall as mountains
and they
fall like fountains
invisible frights
pervading

-why am i afraid of what i can't see?

j.p. dove

i've always
felt alone
yet
i've never
been alone
and
i've always
been myself
but
i've never
felt myself
so
here i am

alone

and by

myself

-*though i'm surrounded by people*

climb and chasm

absent yet present
emotions are like ghost limbs
once there and now gone

-do i still feel?

as i sit below these poor forgotten foxgloves
i feel flawed by this cracked and crooked spine
infinitely splitting in two pieces, yet
never allowing my body to relax

everything is falling down
but i'm welcoming the rains
buoyed by hopes and dreams
as the oceans whisper their pains
summoning ghosts of mermaids
searching for silent siren screams

dark days slip into dank shadows
frosted fragments of soft velvet creams
and the last rays of the golden sun
harnessed by the harvest moon

i'm summer's dying wishes
lost searching for the sea
and its sacred offerings

leaves float idly by yet brittled when i touch
i've lost my heart to autumn's beautiful paintings
and its caramel-scented chaos

and so, i drift into an amber-tinged dream
beneath this enigmatic foxglove
humbled and tired

-to find where i am inspired

its pointy teeth
sunken deeply
within the flesh
of my patience

its collapsing veins
woven tightly
between
the brittleness
of my bones

its powerful grasp
fierce and unmoving
encases itself completely
within my hollow chest

my silent plight pines
aching for release
from the eerie claws
of battling addiction

-please help me

j.p. dove

    emotions like rain
    fall from their eyes
    pleading to the skies
    for torn pages of pain
    to come out again—
    yet there hope lies
    a perfect stain

-misused and abused

when i die, i want to be remembered by
small groups of people who know who i am
for the love i've shared and gifted away
as someone who never expected return
and always graciously accepted embrace

i don't want to be immortalized
by those who know not who i am
but only what i've done
or what i've written

who know i've lived
but haven't stood
beside me

i want to live forevermore
in the hearts i've touched
and leave the rest **aching**
for the chance they never took

i don't want to live on—*lifeless*
in lonely, untouched pages
rotting—on dusty shelves

-no, not in a book

j.p. dove

i said nothing
because
that's all
i felt

-though i do feel empty

love imparted upon
such an unworthy soul
yet unconditional

-how can i continue to hope?

a picturesque gnawing away
of grotesque piles of decay

consequential pestilence
via human malevolence

-the elegy of society

climb and chasm

at many turns
i find myself lost
in the fact that
i'm so much more
than this body

-*beyond flesh*

j.p. dove

let me tell you
about myself
instead of
deciding
for me

-forever misconstrued

the axis

the axis

leaves turn shades of yellow
and the air begins to cool
animals seem to mellow
the lake's an icy pool

fall is nature's reset
to shed the year's past
memories we frequent
release into the vast

expanse of mother earth
our walls are wearing thin
learning your own worth
is growth that begins within

-resetting with nature

a deep connection is a chance meeting
between lost souls' silent retreating
all-knowing truth behind the eyes
beginning anew with endearing apprise

-but where is depth found?

j.p. dove

never kiss feet
that walk on you

*-or you'll simply be
a stepping stone*

to alter your mindset is a colossal feat to conquer
if we falter, offset, or take a seat to ponder
we'll halter our cold sweat, and greet sweet sonder

-exploring perspective

my brain is restless from
constant trains of thought
whistling along tracks
of ever-firing neurons
until coal smoke billows
around my face like the
shroud that surrounds
tedious considerations

perilous derailment
peers from the corner
of that rusted engine
a red lever beckons me
inscribed with the words
"pull brake to stop"

it was then i knew
i'm not the conductor
simply the assistant

and the truth is:
it's okay to rest now
because one doesn't
need to steer a train

-you're simply along for the ride

heavy eyes fluttered
always weighed down
by others' energy
but today
have been beautifully
brought back to life

-dilated and delighted

to ponder is to wander
as thought can be wrought
but
be kinder than your blinder
for restraint is not constraint

-control of self

i f l o a t t h r o u g h l i f e

meandering with eternal demise
be twee n bro ke n te eth
(: around corners in smiles :)

beside deeply carved ruts
over bloodied scrapes and cuts
through an ocean of eyes and
dreams that lay beneath
love's eternal isles

swinging
as high as i once did
when i was a kid
the sky grips my toes
and holds me tight

head back, not from woes
but by my power
and my light

i let my hands off at the top—
never letting fun stop
and jump

i'm falling
as free as a cloud

will i ever reach the ground?

i don't want to know
but if i have to
i'd ask myself

why'd you ever stop reaching for the sky?

and i'd tell the mirror—

i don't know, but i want to try

so, i will
until i'm six feet below
and riddled with worms

-*i'll try and i'll try and i'll try*

i don't want to be scared
but i'm reluctant
to take the chance
to shove fear away
for it has kept me safe

-but at what cost?

gridlock

intersecting lines of thought

(parked)
in the middle   of the road

horns   horns
    blaring from every side

stop
and you'll never go

go
but you'll never stop

neither?
then you'll never know

-*where will i go?*

petrichor floats in through the open door
somehow it tickles the base of my skull
like the way a scent reminds you of the time

before your grandparents died
before you smoked that first cigarette
before you lost your innocence
forgotten that person's name
or tasted your last raindrop

for me:
neapolitan wafer cookies and messy bird cages
juniper or evergreen trees and anything minty
church perfume and a certain candle's
fragrance i can't quite remember

then there's petrichor
the smell of the earth after it rains
its calming, cooling effect pours over me
like thousands of memories flashing before my eyes

i see where every drop lands on the ground
where it's nourishing the soil underneath
and washing my tears away into
tiny glimpses of cycles anew

-so my worries can once again
become my inspirations

j.p. dove

dreams are glances into alternate lives
nightmares are horror scenes with bloody knives
but both offer advice and insight

seams tear between dimensions
relaxing mental and muscle tensions
as you close your eyes
and say goodnight

-with restful intentions

occasionally i dream
of all the places
i've never seen

sometimes i cry
about all the dreams
i've never been

-the seesaw of hope

to take away all the love they've given
was just another way to say, "goodbye"

to give away all the love they've taken
was just another way to say, "hello"

but to compromise—is love unencumbered
by irrational thought and endless worry

prioritize care, courtesy, compassion
and never rush through life in hurry

because it's always harder when
you lead with hurt and fury

so, coat check egos at the door
and communicate instead of bury

-progression

someone can only know
as much as you allow

-but how will i learn to trust again?

perhaps i had just forgotten
this feeling of numbness

somehow lost in trauma's weight
buried by tangible emotions

but the funny thing is:
i really thought i didn't feel
anything anymore

at all

*-but numb **is** something*

the ascent

in silence they suffocated and love felt coerced
confined souls strung with pain—desire unrehearsed
fissured surfaces quake when energy is unearthed anew
to embrace self-love, for their spirits to break through

they set aside iron chains cast from self-doubt
a decision made with love and shared throughout
amid bravery, courage, and with all their might
they climbed atop vulnerability's daring height

vast scars may remain, yet teach survival
but don't fear the reflection of affection
for within their souls' rushing revival
true solace found *imperfection*

-*unchained introspection*

don't wait up anymore
i've learned my lesson

i don't follow footsteps
that can't walk in mine

-i've worn yours

j.p. dove

today
i cannot
hold hands
with happiness
until i allow
my grasp
on past
freed

-you need to let go

dependent on where you are
our viewpoints are relative

when time is bent and warped
reality becomes subjective

strong magnetism begets
hidden mechanisms of change

positivity, like light
travels through nothing

how strange?

-theory of positivity

the ebb and flow of what's given and taken
is far too often disastrously forsaken

day by day, they've given all they've got
hearts once softened, now contorted in knots

you're told to please others before yourself
but to appease another is to sit on the shelf

knots, now loose, begin to unfold
hearts, once taut, no longer fit the mold

you must be selfish, but please stay selfless
to see self-love through these new lenses

-selflesh

a voice once lost
now regained again
a benevolent cost
to maintain a friend

we must reach out
to offer a hand
to condemn clout
and to understand

we know not
what others live
but you may want
a hand to give

-we can change

as true as time shall pass, our hearts elate
a powerful connection we do share
a bond so pure and found beyond compare
a belief in love at its purest state

with sudden quakes of fear and twists of fate
we weather stormy seas with hope and care
in every trial, love's light we declare
our lives entwined, no distance can abate

in peaceful seconds, love will rise
through life's obstacles, brightly as the sun
in muttered hopes and dreams below the skies
a strength that binds us when the phantoms run

together, chasing all that love defies
a bond, a bastion, broken by no one

-infinite affinity

find your light
in each passing second
reach out for it with both hands
adorn the crown upon your mind
blend its beams into your canvas
hear its echo from mountaintops

celebrate success as though it's here
until you become the rays you seek
send them soaring into the heavens
toward sun and moon in harmony

reactions become the ocean
drawn in by lunar forces
breaking against your shores
only to retreat in calm release
a gentle letting go of negativity

shadows grow tall and stretch
as days melt softly into night
brisk winds caress your skin
and you soar across the sky

-*like the light you've always been*

to love ourselves
we must be *forgiving*

to enjoy ourselves
we must be *present*

but to *be* ourselves
we must learn **our self**

-it's the first step

if each day is brighter than the last
then every word you say is a letter to your past
remember the strength you've worked to amass
and how a simple smile can outlast your mask

for within you lies a spark, your truest self
patiently waiting on an inner shelf
it's longing to be set free—

to release holds and untie knots
to smooth the folds; to connect thoughts
to overflow molds with the love you've got

clearing the rot means embracing the bold
cherishing what's sought is letting go of the old

so, cool the hot or warm the cold
beat those pots and tarnish that gold

because we fought to be told that
who we are is *not* masked

for our facades concealed far more
than we were **ever** asked

-***authenticism***

there are so many words inside my mind
tucked away, hidden, impossible to find
yet i've begun to delve, to unearth the past
to uncover why my voice was silenced so fast
by self-doubt and endless worries

anxiety.
fear.
trauma.

bittersweet, poignant vortices

to write these thoughts means reliving the pain
obligates peeling masks to find face again
it demands truth and apologies made
boundaries set, no longer afraid

it commands me to move without regret
to rise from society's ashes and never forget

though i will cry, and hatred may sting
*i'll grow into love, **i'll find my wings***
for shaping my fate, through toil and strife
is how i'll forge a new path to life

-i'm making my dreams reality

dear outsider,

you claim that
you love the addict
when they're producing
when they don't affect you
when they choose to help you
but
when all they're able to create
is self-loathed misery to all
you choose to hate them
you choose to neglect
you choose not to
help them or
even call

but their most pure and true desires
are people who are there to listen
to the pieces they are missing
and to be themselves again
as best as they can
so, they learn
as you do
or can

that *only* with our love
will we erase the hate
only with that love
we learn to create
only with love
you change
their fate

-*only with love*
the addict is freed

soft hands are timeworn and
rough where calluses have formed
yet they caress lovingly

-in weathered embrace

climb and chasm

truth transforms transference
to triumphant togetherness

think therapeutic thunderstorms
take thy thoughtful tolerance

time talks tender tempos
tougher than temptation

tranquil treasures teeming
through trifling tribulation

-transcending

to love someone who loves you forever
is a gift all should know

but

to miss someone who can't miss you
is a pain all its own

and

to be someone who loves themselves
is a journey full of growth, so

together

we're the ones who will start to change
all it is we've ever known

-hand in hand

your mind's my compass
always looking up

magnetized toward becoming
choice editions of ourselves

i look forward to
taking the time
it takes to see

all we become
and everything
we hope we'll be

-i'm never lost with you

it's true—ignorance is bliss
but intelligence, alas
has fallen amiss

for what is our experience
our lives, this fleeting dance
without the wonder
of at least

attempting a glance?

-the dance of comprehension

the apex

the apex

j.p. dove

as the sky folds in
on itself, like origami
i sink into its pressure
as if its fingers caress me
like square clouds of paper

i thank the sky
for not creasing me
for being here

for shaping me
into a version
of myself

i find quite beautiful

-delicate strain

earth's magnetism jostles my compass
rendering me unsure of where to go
residual nightmares of parental *guidance*
flood my already anxious heart
with an overwhelming flutter

i'm stuck at a fork in the road—
though i'm not sure why it's called a fork
when there are only ever two options:

do or **don't**

i remember four prongs on this utensil
sometimes three for a salad—but never two?
though there are seven paths in my road
and i can't even tell which way is up
or how to get to the ground

i feel ground, like coffee beans
brewed then poured out
but have you heard of grounding?
feet bare, pressed against sacred soil
as if the earth could *pulse* me into myself

but i can barely put one foot
in front of the other
let alone take off my shoes

j.p. dove

i'm searching for the synchronization
of my brain, body, and soul
yet i find reasons in my mind deterring
me from the winding trail of olive trees
extending the peace and friendship i long for

inside my soul, i gaze upon fears
that have bound my legs in chains of
fury and unwarranted responses for years
since long before i couldn't crawl away
from their ghoulish grasp

my tormented being holds onto
mental and physical strife
when demons roamed freely
but i'm taking back my life

my fears have turned inward
terrified of the only person
capable of vanquishing them

me

for when fears meet acceptance,
healing, and understanding,
their hold weakens, and

-i grow stronger.

climb and chasm

when forgiveness and love are present
demons sit across from trauma—

a cacophony of beatings and screams
thunder through caverns in my chest
echoes of past, present, and future
fill the space inside my fragile ribs

but as they sit, they converse
encaged in grips of rational thought
and forced to reconcile their disparities

fears now only whisper warnings they were meant to:

a skipped step, a sudden turn,
a false promise, or a red flag.

when trauma is rendered paralyzed
astounded by anxiety's departure
i'm filled with relief and acceptance—
no longer forced to stand guard

and soon, i will macerate my demons
i will turn my false fears into dust
i will fill my hollow bones
with strength i've always carried

as my body relaxes
rusted chains will be broken
my soul will breathe
scarred emotions will heal

my toughened exterior will soften
as my heart is mended and sewn
like the unique patterns of a quilt—
each a polaroid of captured moments
threading time with thimbled thoughts

then, i will finally realize
that every lovely fragment
has *always* fit together *perfectly*
i'll accept it's okay not to be okay
as long as i am me—unapologetically

-*i will*

life doesn't *just* have meaning
life *is* our meaning
and **love** is our
purpose
♥

-discovering the secret

eyes of different hues
met in silent gaze
two are golden brown
the others ocean green

brightly lit whenever around
and twinkled when they're told
of all the wonder and amazement
within each other they've unfold

a language spoken without words
a connection beyond the surface
a shared moment of intimacy
a shining sparkle of deeper purpose

their mind and soul are one, together
for their light and warmth is strong

oh, how special, and how sweet
is their shared invisible bond!

strokes of luck like these
are nearly rare as diamonds

a partnership so sacred
you'd do anything to find it

-golden and green

climb and chasm

another day is upon us
a wonderful chance is given
to do better than we have before
because we've foreseen new visions
where we're free to roam, to explore,
and to abandon our inhibitions
today, we form purpose
and now, we control
our dispositions

-metamorphosis

j.p. dove

oh, how i've grown; oh, how i've healed
no longer have my eyes in pain been sealed
my lungs freely breathe, in vain no longer burned
my tears are dry, minds' fears unlearned

my heart no longer aches with lust
and i no longer smile as if i must
my teeth are clean; bed is made
my fight is seen; anger fades

the dishes done; the laundry stowed
i now find joy in words bestowed
boundaries set; self-worth on show
no longer will stray winds blow

remember when you begged for change?
oh my, you've changed

-look how much you've changed...

climb and chasm

anger is blind and destructive
and assumptions are asses
embarrassment hides away
while fear lurks in the shadows
sadness quietly shuts the door
and weeps all over the floor

as guilt draws the shades
pride slams the window open
and regret begets confusion
envy ends friendships
as anxiety and jealousy can

so, curiosity peers inside
and courage builds new bridges
while empathy kneels beside compassion
to extend understanding's hand
to frustration and nostalgia

who're thumbing through old photos
with longing, desire, wonder, and awe
loneliness is sitting there, too
playing with finger puppets—alone

j.p. dove

then, trust walks in with gratitude
excitement can't stand still
love comes in to hold you
to comb its fingers through your hair

while joy draws everyone in
hope promises happier tomorrows
as relief exhales again
and burden relaxes its weight

until finally, passion is allowed
a dance with bliss and euphoria
and satisfaction blows a sigh

shock and amazement's eyes widen
when optimism is accepted
and anguish blossoms
into serenity

resilience stands in the doorway
as calmness and peace grab the glass
acceptance wraps everyone in its arms
and whispers, "we are one, even in fragments"

-and healing begins its work

along that forgotten highway
their backs lay windswept
like broken blades of grass

they slumber dreamily
through each passing cloud
and its transformations

their faces grew wrinkles
hands and demeanors
softened to silk

no longer angry at the sun
but comforted by its beams
as it shines its pearly whites
and the grass grows

-beneath the sun's smile

your mind is worth knowing
your kindness worth showing

with your heart on your mind
and your mind in your heart

you will prevail

you will succeed

-in finding strength within

one day
all we'll be
is ink on paper
and *electricity*
in the sky

-be present

j.p. dove

i used to think about
how strange it is
to be here
now i know
we're just strange
and happen to be here

-to think

each breathe surges
like waves to the shore
a voice within emerges
lighting me forevermore

a singular star blesses the moon
companionship in solitude

dear houser of light,

*beam me through
dark forgotten waters*

guide me past
obstacles on my flight

and pierce the fog
in these lonely skies

*-for my voice is my lighthouse:
as i navigate the night*

forest green leaves sway
painted across lush landscape
rustled by rushing eastern winds
baby blue skies are swirling watercolors
mingling with the entrails of my
old, wizened paint brush

a soft, warm sun invites me
toward unfamiliar highs
drawing ever closer

my banks of safety crumble—
waves of new crash and roll, retreating
sands grasp onto my pruned fingers
twinkling stars guide my gait
as oceans stalk the moon

then, night awakens
stumbling into the room
its harrowed eyes gawping
piercing my humbled soul

nocturnal spirits rise
whispering secret longing
yearning only to
seduce the sun

to resurrect light from darkness
to unveil spark and rekindle flame
a fusion of inferno and shade
where doubt is lost

-but i remain

dear future me,

i marvel in curiosity
over who you've become

have you conquered your fears?
have you liberated your negativity?

do you still wonder about me, or
what you could've done differently?

are you satiated,
or completely overborne?

wherever you are
whoever you are

-i hope you're at ease,
and i hope you're free

j.p. dove

truth be told
among years of discord
i've begun to love myself

courageously bringing
a *half-full* cup to the table

a place i've sat before
to drink the years' past

but i no longer see
the cup *half-empty*

my cup is full

-*a toast to self-love*

about this poetry collection

climb and chasm is a passion project,
an act of dedication, crafted with care,
tracing the continuum of human experience—
from the depths of despair to the heights of hope,
and for all the lights breaking through the shadows.

this collection is an exploration of my heart's journey,
a weaving of quiet reflections and fierce truths,
crafted to be felt, to resonate, and to linger.

it unfolds in four stages of progression:
the abyss, the axis, the ascent, and the apex—
each taking you on a trip through your most
complex and difficult emotions.

climb and chasm provokes raw thought:
anger, anxiety, happiness, and love.
prepare for soul-searching as we
search for lost souls, together.

because together, ***we are one.***

about the author

J.P. Dove is a poet, entrepreneur, and creative mind who is drawn to the quiet power of transformation. Through his work, he explores the depths and heights of human emotion, capturing reflections lingering in both the shadows
and the light that follows them.

J.P. is a neurodivergent person who enjoys life in Oregon, and prefers to spend his time writing in his nook,
looking at the stars, going antiquing,
or reading poetry!

Together with his partner, Tionna, they create art imbued with intention and compassion for the planet, transforming upcycling into an act of renewal. Their small business, Terpy Treasures, is a heartfelt endeavor dedicated to blending artistry with sustainability, giving materials a second life.

Their Yorkie-Poo, Doobie-Doo, is the heart of their home. As a gentle soul, he reminds them to cherish the simple times in life. For them, Doobie is more than a pet; he's family and the best teacher of joy and presence they could ask for.

In *climb and chasm,* J.P. invites readers on a journey through love, loss, and self-discovery. He hopes these words offer a space to pause, to feel deeply, and to find echoes of one's own travels—knowing that even in solitude,

we are never truly alone.

dear readers,

this may be the end of the first, but it's also the first of many; thank you for walking with me through these pages.

this collection is a true labor of my love for poetry.
each word, every line, carries a piece of my bleeding heart; a quiet hope it may become something meaningful in your hands.

thank you for allowing my words to rest there,
at your fingertips, and for letting them settle into your thoughts.
this journey is no longer mine alone, but a thread we share—
woven through the quiet spaces, the depths of the abysmal,
the peaks of the hopeful, and those places in between.
it's a thread that binds not only these pages,
but all who hold this book, and i hope it
becomes larger than i could imagine.

i hope you've found pieces of yourself here, ones that heal,
resonate, or give you courage. i hope you carry them with
bravery, with tenderness, and as your companions.

this book exists only because you choose to read it,
to breathe life into it, and to feel it as it was meant to be felt.
for your presence, your strength, and your willingness
to walk with me through this, i am endlessly grateful.

may this book be the beginning of many shared pages,
as we continue to seek, find, and create meaning
in the words that connect us all.

with all of my love,

-*j.p. dove*

www.ingramcontent.com/pod-product-compliance
Lightning Source LLC
Chambersburg PA
CBHW071200090426
42736CB00012B/2401